Chicago, Illinois

Behind the News | **CLIMATE CHANGE**: Is the World in Danger **?**

GARY E. BARR

© 2007 Heinemann Library
a division of Reed Elsevier Inc.
Chicago, Illinois

Customer Service 888-454-2279
Visit our website at www.heinemannraintree.com

Designed by David Poole and Kamae Design
Printed and bound in China by South China
Printing Company

11 10 09 08 07
10 9 8 7 6 5 4 3 2 1

Library of Congress Cataloging-in-Publication Data

Barr, Gary, 1951-
  Climate change / Gary E. Barr.
    p. cm. -- (Behind the news)
  Includes bibliographical references and index.
  ISBN 1-4034-8830-4 (library binding)
  1-4034-9353-7 (pbk)
  1. Climatic changes--Juvenile literature. 2.
Climatic changes--Environmental aspects--Juvenile
literature. 3. Nature--Effect of human
beings on--Juvenile literature. I. Title. II. Series:
Behind the news
(Chicago, Ill.)
  QC981.8.C5B393 2006
  551.6--dc22
                                      2006016830

The paper used to print this book comes from
sustainable resources.

Disclaimer

Acknowledgements

The publishers would like to thank the following
for permission to reproduce photographs:
Alamy Images p. 49 (Transtock Inc./Guy
Spangenberg); Corbis pp. 5 (Corbis/Craig
Lovell), 7 (Gerald Favre/Geologos), 8 (Claudia
Daut/Reuters), 11 (Shepard Sherbell/SABA), 13
(Pitchal Frederic/Sygma), 15, 16 (Jim Sugar),
19, 25 (David Ball), 26 (Brad Loper/Dallas
Morning News), 28, 29, 32 (James Davis; Eye
Ubiquitous), 33 (William Findlay), 37 (Danny
Lehman), 38, 40 (Kevin Lamarque/Reuters), 46
(Raymond Gehman), 47 (Pizzoli Alberto); Empics
pp. 17 (Volodymyr Repik/AP), 20 (Batchelo
Barry Batchelor/AP), 39 (Michel Euler/AP), 42
(Ian Barrett/AP); Getty Images pp. 14 (News),
18 (Photodisc), 23 (Photodisc), 31 (Photodisc),
34 (Photodisc); photos.com p. 36; Science Photo
Library pp. 45 (US GEOLOGICAL SURVEY), 48 (D.
Van Ravenswaay); The Kobal Collection p. 7 (20th
Century Fox).

Cover photograph of dry ground, reproduced with
permission of Still Pictures (Paul Stattery/UNEP).

The author and Publishers gratefully acknowledge
the publications from which the longer written
sources in the book are drawn. In some cases
the wording or sentence structure has been
simplified to make the material appropriate for
a school readership:

Robert Marquand (in the *Christian Science
Monitor*) p.4; New York Times p.18; Robert
Socolow (in *Scientific American*) p.12; *Sydney
Morning Herald* p.22.

CONTENTS

Any words appearing in the text in bold, **like this**, are explained in the Glossary.

A CHANGE OF CLIMATE?

"Flood Wrecks Ancient Monastery"

In 1999 a 1,000-year-old Buddhist monastery in Ladakh, India, was badly damaged by flooding. **Climatologists** believe the flood resulted from **global warming** melting glaciers in the Himalayas. A *Christian Science Monitor* article from November 5, 1999 reported the Ladakh monastery disaster. In this article Kathleen McGinty, a chemist who led the U.S. Council of Environmental Quality, said: "We can't say that **greenhouse gases** are the main reason. But we can say that the melt is consistent with a global pattern that marks the signature of **climate change**."

In the same article, a climatologist from Delhi, India (who requested not to be identified), disagreed: "These glacial data are early warnings and need to be taken seriously. But the boundaries of glaciers are never fixed. They recede, but they also expand. It is far too early to judge."

Who is right?

The story of the monastery flood is one of many to raise people's concerns. Arguments go back and forth. The Delhi climatologist said there are too many "exaggerations" of data and that we should not be alarmed. Experts such as geologist Joseph Wadia, however, say it is not normal for glaciers to suddenly begin melting. Some experts say a major flood after 1,000 years of no flooding indicates drastic changes in climate.

Syeda Sajeda Chowdhury, Bangladesh's Minister for Environment and Forests, said that nearly 20 percent of her country could be under water in 15 years if global warming is not controlled. Yet this article in the *Christian Science Monitor* was one of the only articles written about the Ladakh event.

Are newspapers and people ignoring stories about global warming and its tragic implications? Is air pollution causing the world's climate to change? Is the world in danger?

The hillside positions of monasteries, such as this one in the Ladakh province of northern India, usually protects them. However, warmer climatic conditions have led to powerful flash floods in recent years.

DISAPPEARING GLACIERS

For years now, glaciers from Patagonia to the Swiss Alps have been watched for signs of melting because of greenhouse gases and the effects of global warming. In South Asia the question is not if the ice is melting, but how fast. According to studies by the International Commission for Snow and Ice, "Glaciers in the Himalayas are receding faster than in any other part of the world . . . If the present rate continues, the likelihood of them disappearing by the year 2035 is very high."

Storms, floods, and destruction?

Storms, floods, and destruction: Does this sound like a title for an exciting movie about natural disasters? It is actually a prediction made by some scientists. Most scientists agree that climate change is happening, and at a fairly rapid pace. A few scientists disagree and say that climate change is natural, safe, and will be gradual.

Many opinions

There are many different predictions for the next 100 years. These range from several coastal cities being completely flooded to almost no change in ocean levels. Some scientists say global warming will cause Earth to become a "hot planet," while others say it will cause a premature **ice age**. Destructive "super hurricanes," flooding, and **pandemics** will increase according to some experts, while other climatologists say this is unlikely.

A key question in the climate change debate is how much effect human actions are having. Most scientists agree that global industrialization is affecting climate, but there is great disagreement about how much this is altering the world's climate. Some experts disagree over whether humans are causing significant climate changes. However, almost all scientists say that climate is changing at a fairly rapid pace. There are many differing opinions about climate change among experts, and much still to learn. What should the public believe?

There are a number of large climate studies being done right now. Massive amounts of money and teams of scientists around the world are studying climate change. As a future taxpayer, how much time and money do you think should be spent on these studies?

Movies vs. science

Adding to confusion about climate change are movies such as *Waterworld* and *The Day After Tomorrow*. Both are extreme in their views and present scenes that could not happen, according to almost all experts. In *Waterworld* the polar ice caps have completely melted, raising ocean levels so high that few land areas are left. Scientists estimate that a very small percentage of Earth would be covered if this really occurred. In *The Day After Tomorrow* global warming causes huge storms and ice-age conditions. The storms shown in the movie are far too destructive. It would take hundreds of years for temperatures to cause the conditions that occur within 30 days in the movie.

Glacial formations like this one in Iceland reveal information about climate change. Scientists gather samples from ice that formed thousands of years ago. They look at how rocks and tiny organisms are embedded to learn about past climates.

THREE MISCONCEPTIONS

Misconceptions are views and opinions that are incorrect, although many people may believe them to be true. Here are three misconceptions about global warming:

1. MISCONCEPTION: In the movie *Waterworld*, global warming causes so much flooding that almost no dry land remains. THE TRUTH: If all of the ice on Earth melted, ocean levels would rise by around 262 feet (80 meters).
2. MISCONCEPTION: Launching rockets into space causes global warming. THE TRUTH: Rocket launches have almost no effect on global warming.
3. MISCONCEPTION: Serious global warming can cause only warmer temperatures. THE TRUTH: There is evidence that the processes currently causing global warming could one day lead to an ice age.

The climate report

What is the difference between climate and weather? Weather includes short-term atmospheric conditions, while climate is long-term, average weather. Weather conditions are determined by short-term air pressure conditions, wind directions, temperatures, and **humidity** in the air.

Weather changes daily. Worldwide, one of the most frequently asked questions each morning is: "What will the weather be like today?" People need to know how to dress and what activities might be affected by the weather. For those who work outside, knowing if it will rain on a particular day can be very important.

Climate is weather over a long period of time. Climatologists can predict a place's climate if they know annual averages in temperature and **precipitation**. These are the most important measurements for both weather and climate. Changes in climate normally occur in a gradual way, over a very long period of time.

Cuba's top meteorologist, Jose Rubiera, points to a map of his country. Cuba is prone to powerful tropical storms and hurricanes. This makes weather reports crucial to the safety and well-being of Cuba's citizens.

Rainfall and temperature variations

Climatologists define deserts as places with less than 10 inches (25 centimeters) of annual precipitation. Tropical rainforests get over 80 inches (2 meters) per year. Precipitation amounts are pretty predictable, but winds, evaporation rates, and other factors can cause slight variations.

Climatic temperatures are more complicated. In places such as Hawaii, annual average temperatures vary only a few degrees, from 72 to 76 °F (22 to 24 °C). It is easy to classify this as a warm place. Most places near oceans do not experience big seasonal differences in temperature. This is because water temperatures do not change as quickly as land temperatures.

Other places, however, vary quite a lot in temperature. Verkhoyansk, Russia, has annual averages of 60 °F (15 °C) in summer and –50 °F (–45 °C) in winter. This is one of the widest seasonal variations on Earth. Some deserts experience 24-hour temperature swings from 100 °F (37 °C) during daylight hours to 32 °F (0 °C) during the night. These wide variations make it difficult to use temperatures to predict the year-round climate of a place.

Climate change involves gradual trends that normally span hundreds, or even thousands, of years. An example of a quick change in climate is an event that occurred 11,000 years ago. During this era, North America's average temperature dropped 9 °F (5 °C) in a 40-year period—a significant decrease!

Other variables
Prevailing winds are winds that consistently blow in a certain direction. Wind speed and direction have a major effect on rainfall and temperature. Likewise, how far a place is from an ocean, the location of high mountains nearby, and the **height** of a place can all affect the type of climate that is present.

TEMPERATURES THROUGH HISTORY

The line shows how Earth's average temperatures have repeated themselves over the past 400,000 years.

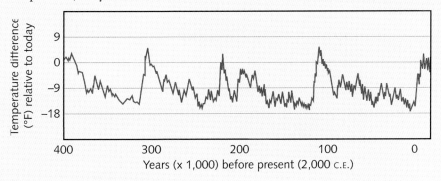

The importance of climate

We all want to know about weather every day, but climate also has an important effect on our lives. One of the reasons people live where they do, and live as they do, is because of climatic conditions.

Choosing where to live

If a person visited northern Siberia in summer, he or she might find the daytime temperature was 60 °F (15 °C). Would it be a wise decision to move there permanently because the person liked the weather on that day? The person would be disappointed if he or she moved expecting warm temperatures every day. Northern Siberia has long, very cold winters with many daily temperatures below −30 °F (−34 °C). Temperatures of around 60 °F (15 °C) would be rare.

In developed nations, people think about their occupation and the friends and family they want to be near when they are deciding where to live. Work and family are two important factors, but climate type is also important to their decision. Do people want to live in a place with year-round warm temperatures, a place with beautiful changes in the seasons, or a place that gets lots of snow? Everyone has his or her own preference, but climate can be a major factor in a person's choice of location.

Climate also determines what types of plants and animals will be present and how people will live their lives. People who live near the Sahara Desert lead very different lives from people living in the high mountain valleys of the Himalayas. They eat different foods, dress differently, have very different shelters, and do outdoor jobs in very different ways.

Climate limits the places where we can live. There are several land areas on Earth that are too cold for human habitation. Antarctica, for example, has a changing population of researchers and scientists, but no permanent residents. High mountains are too cold for people to live on and are prone to destructive storms. Large deserts make human habitation difficult because of the lack of water. Areas such as rainforests simply have unpleasant climatic conditions: extremely high humidity, intense heat, and strong thunderstorms.

Climate even affects how and where people build their houses. Bangladesh, in South-Central Asia, is a nation prone to massive flooding. This climatic problem forces people to live in houses on stilts and in parts of the nation with higher elevation. If they do not do this, they risk losing their homes— and even their lives.

Climate types

To give people a description of a place's climate, scientists came up with a method for combining annual temperature and precipitation averages into "climate types." Climatologists identify 12 basic climates on Earth. For example, Verkhoyansk in Russian Siberia is located in a subarctic climate zone. "Subarctic" means dominated by cold temperatures and lower-than-average annual precipitation. Parts of Hawaii are in a "humid tropical" climate zone. "Humid" means above-average precipitation and "tropical" means warm year-round.

If a person understands the characteristics of each climate type, looking at a "climate map" can provide helpful information. People can identify places covered by harsh deserts, places where skiing may be good, or the best places to find warm beaches. Scientists depend on detailed studies to produce such good climate maps.

Would you like to live here, in Surgut, Russia? Some people love snow and cold weather, but most people choose to live in places with more moderate temperatures than Siberian Russia.

Prove it

Scientific articles are usually written differently from news reports. Scientific articles are written in a way to show a great deal of information, often the results of experiments or studies. Below is a headline and opening paragraph from a general newspaper article, followed by a scientific article. Notice how much information and statistical data is contained in the scientific article compared to the news report . . .

The world after 9/11

"On September 11, 2001, the 21st century was born. If, as the historian Eric Hobsbawm has suggested, the 20th century really began with the assassination in Sarajevo that sparked the First World War, it is fair to suggest that, in the impact it has already had on the shape of our era, the 21st century began with the demolition of the World Trade Center."

News report from the *Deccan* [India] *Herald*, January 22, 2004

"Can we bury global warming?"

"When Shakespeare took a breath, 280 molecules out of every million entering his lungs were **carbon dioxide**. Each time you draw a breath today, 380 molecules per million are carbon dioxide. That portion climbs about two molecules every year [...] Scientists know that carbon dioxide is warming the atmosphere, which in turn is causing the sea level to rise, and that the CO_2 absorbed by the ocean is acidifying the water. But they are unsure of exactly how climate could alter across the globe [...]"

Scientific article from *Scientific American*, July 2005

Writing about scientific studies

Articles on climate and other scientific topics usually include detailed statistics. It is a writer's job to arrange this data in a meaningful way. Tables, charts, and diagrams are very useful because they can show scientific information in a brief but informative manner.

Can we trust the **media**? Very few journalists report facts that they know to be untrue, but they cannot be expected to have expert knowledge about cutting-edge scientific research. It is especially important for them to find expert sources that are not only reliable, but that can also communicate technical information in an understandable way. Journalists often have to trust the information they are given by scientists. Like everyone else, scientists can make mistakes, so there is always a chance that some information will be inaccurate.

A meteorologist is hard at work. Meteorologists use scientific techniques to study and predict the weather. They often study detailed map representations of wind direction, air pressure readings, and radar images of clouds.

It is possible to present the news in different ways. An article in a magazine intended for the business world is likely to present a different **slant** on a story than a magazine devoted to promoting environmental issues. Many newspapers, magazines, news services, and Internet sites also have a political **bias**. That means they might be more willing to support a government's view of an issue, for example, or always be against it.

There are also different kinds of journalist. Some journalists give on-the-spot reports of news events. Their reports are usually short and might not have much background detail. Other journalists investigate the news. Investigative journalists do lots of research to try to discover the facts behind a news story. They may have more time to interview experts on each side and try to cover all the aspects of a story. Their articles, known as features, are often longer.

Some feature articles highlight one particular point of view. Articles that express a personal viewpoint are generally known as opinion pieces or editorials. These articles may contain a long interview with one or two individuals, quoting their opinions on a subject. A journalist may also choose to express his or her own personal views on a subject.

There are numerous climate studies being carried out around the world. How these studies are reported in the media helps us to understand climate change.

A tree fell in the forest

"Very old and wide-spread is the opinion that forests have an important impact on rainfall. . . . If forests enhance the amount and frequency of precipitation simply by being there, deforestation [removal of trees] as part of agricultural expansion everywhere, must necessarily result in less rainfall and more frequent droughts." This quote came from a German scientist named Eduard Brückner. He believed that the destruction of forests would mean less rainfall and more droughts. Brückner's theory was that humans were changing Earth's climate. He wrote this in 1890!

Human impacts on climate change were discovered a long time ago. Unfortunately, the media largely ignored climate change as a significant story for many years. If a huge tree falls in the forest, does it make a sound? Yes. If a story is very important, does it always make the headlines? The answer is no. Nature controls sound, but people control headlines.

Some people believe that science is a boring subject. For this reason many significant scientific articles are not published in newspapers or are "buried" inside them where few people will notice. Brückner was an important scientist, but few of his writings were published.

For years people ignored stories about climate change. Recent concerns about the effects of global warming have led to a dramatic increase in public interest. Here, reporters question Alexander Downer, Australia's Minister for Foreign Affairs, about a climate conference he attended.

The combination of drought and misuse of the land led to devastating dust storms such as this one in Texas, in 1935.

Why stories get published

When newspapers and other media decide not to print scientific stories, it is often a financial decision. Most media sources seek maximum profits by attracting large numbers of readers. If a story is seen as boring, it will not sell newspapers. The media publish articles they think the public wants to read.

From 1890 all the way to the 1970s, very few stories on climate change received attention. An exception was in the 1930s, when **Dust Bowl** conditions forced many people from the midwestern United States to flee their homes. Kansas, Oklahoma, and Texas were hardest hit. Years of drought conditions, combined with soil erosion caused by poor farming methods, left huge areas unsuitable for growing crops. For a time, the topics of climate and climate change appeared several times as prominent news items. This attention, however, did not last.

Television coverage

In the 1970s, extreme droughts and **desertification** were cause for concern among scientists. The public became interested, but the world's media again gave the stories little attention. In 1974 an expert named Nigel Calder gained enough support to make the first major television program on the possible effects of global warming. Few people saw it because it was shown as an educational program, rather than as an important news item.

Increased attention

From the 1970s to the 1980s, scientists began to publish more and more articles showing that global warming was taking place. They also showed that human activities, such as burning **fossil fuels** in factories and vehicles, increased global warming. However, little publicity was given to the issue. Finally, in the 1990s the public noticed winters were warming, politicians began to speak about global warming, and the United Nations increased its efforts to address climate change issues. There was now much more interest in global warming, the **greenhouse effect**, and climate change.

Manabe Syukuro was one of the first meteorologists to explore the possibility that emissions of carbon dioxide and other greenhouse gases could affect climate.

In 1986 a nuclear power plant malfunctioned in Chernobyl, Ukraine. Poisonous gases were released and caused 10,000 deaths. The media, which was government-controlled at the time, tried to mislead and conceal evidence from people because it was embarrassing. This deception probably led to some of the deaths.

IGNORED FOR YEARS

Bias occurs when only one side of a story is told, or when one view of the issue is favored or supported. Bias, combined with the media's need to sell their stories, resulted in some omissions during the 1990s. During these years, the media gave less publicity to scientists who said climate change was due primarily to natural causes. Instead they frequently published "disaster stories" associated with global warming. They did this even though natural causes for climate change had been shown to have a significant impact. Newspapers, television, radio, and magazines knew the disaster stories would "sell" better than ones looking at natural climate changes.

"The Big Melt"

"Many scientists say it has taken a long time for them to accept that global warming, partly the result of carbon dioxide and other heat-trapping gases in the atmosphere, could shrink the Arctic's summer cloak of ice. The particularly sharp warming and melting in the last few decades is thought by many experts to result from a mix of human and natural causes."

This quote comes from an article in the *New York Times* on October 25, 2005. What is the story behind this news?

Polar bears once roamed across huge floating masses of ice to hunt for food. Warmer climatic conditions have caused the ice to shrink and break. This causes great difficulties for polar bears trying to find food.

Shrinking ice caps

In recent years the ice caps have rapidly decreased in size. The Arctic ice cap is thinning at a rate of almost 1 percent each year. The melt rate began to increase dramatically about 40 years ago, and almost half of the cap has melted in that time. Some scientists say the increased melting at the ice caps has been caused by air pollution warming the atmosphere.

Very little land exists near the North Pole. Masses of ice several miles wide and hundreds of feet thick used to cover the region's Arctic Ocean. Now these ice chunks are diminishing, while large water areas between the ice expand.

In 1985 Joseph Farman headed a group of scientists who first noticed a hole in the **ozone layer**. The ozone layer absorbs a great deal of the Sun's heat as rays enter Earth's atmosphere. **CFCs** (cholorofluorocarbons) are man-made substances that damage the ozone layer. They were banned years ago, but the ozone layer is still depleted. The effects are more extreme in polar regions, and this is where the "holes" are that Farman discovered. Lack of ozone increases temperatures at the Poles and is contributing to the polar thaw.

The thawing effects have caused great changes for plants and animals. Polar bears, for example, are at risk because they can no longer find their way across ice to feeding grounds. Some plants are flourishing in places once covered by ice, while others are dying because increased temperatures dry out their normal water supplies.

CARIBOU AND GLOBAL WARMING

Caribou are an example of an animal threatened by warmer climates. Caribou are large antelope that travel many miles to reach pastures they need to feed on to survive. Warm temperatures have brought swarms of mosquitoes to the caribou's grazing areas and driven them to cooler places. Unfortunately, pastures are not as rich in these cooler places, and the caribou are beginning to die out.

"Past Cycles: Ice Age Speculations"

"To understand climate change, the obvious first step would be to explain the colossal coming and going of ice ages . . . paleoclimatologists [climate scientists] succeeded brilliantly, discovering a strangely regular pattern of glacial cycles."

This quote comes from an article that appeared on the American Institute of Physics website in June 2005. What is the story behind this news?

Just like weather, climates change. The changes are much slower, but even small alterations can have huge effects on all living things.

Climate cycles

A cycle is something that repeats itself. **Climate cycles** describe times when Earth has alternated between ice ages and periods of higher-than-average temperatures. These cycles are very gradual, taking thousands of years, but they do cause major changes in Earth's environment. Current concerns are that a future cycle will cause climatic conditions that make it difficult for plants, animals, and humans to survive.

Climatic history warns us that drastic changes can take place. For example, the Sahara Desert used to be a very rainy, heavily forested region. Wind patterns and other climatic conditions changed and turned the region into the world's largest desert. Another example involved dinosaurs. Many scientists now believe that a quick climate change may have contributed to the extinction of dinosaurs.

Scientist Neville Hollingworth found this mammoth skull in Gloucestershire, England. It is believed to be 50,000 years old and dates back to a past ice age. Climatologists believe Earth will have another ice age in the future.

Unpredictable

Climate, climate change, and climate processes taking place in Earth's atmosphere are so complicated that long-range predictions are impossible. Climatologists combine information about the past and the present to make predictions about the future. They try to come up with a **baseline** that describes "average climate" for Earth. They then study what causes Earth's climate to change. By examining the data, they hope to predict future climate trends and find out if humans can prevent catastrophic changes.

Humans and climate cycles

Water vapor is water that has **evaporated** into the atmosphere. It is the dominant greenhouse gas and prevents much of the Sun's heat from reaching Earth's surface. It also keeps heat from escaping from Earth.

Compared to water vapor, carbon dioxide makes up a very small percentage of greenhouse gases. Volcanoes emit much of the carbon dioxide in the atmosphere. Even so, many scientists are worried that carbon dioxide released by human activity may be speeding up climate change. They say human activities, such as the burning of fossil fuels, are having a negative impact on Earth's atmosphere.

A small percentage of scientists say that humans have little impact on climate cycles because most changes occur naturally. Those who see human activity as a threat say current trends in the climate cycle show that humans do have an impact. As the debate goes on, so does human activity, such as burning rainforests to clear space for new agricultural lands.

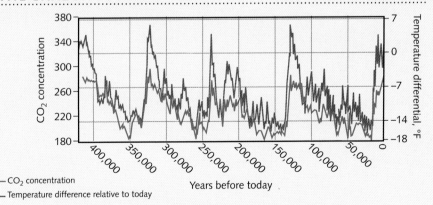

THE CARBON DIOXIDE/TEMPERATURE RELATIONSHIP

— CO₂ concentration
— Temperature difference relative to today

Years before today

This graph shows how the carbon dioxide concentration in the atmosphere and the surface temperature of Earth have changed over the last 400,000 years.

"Too Late to Save Fragile Ecosystems"

"It could be too late to protect some of Australia's most unique ecosystems, such as the Great Barrier Reef and the Daintree Rainforest, from the destructive effects of climate change, according to a report released by the [Australian] Federal Government today."

This quote comes from an article that appeared in the *Sydney Morning Herald* on July 26, 2005. What is the story behind this news?

In most ways, tropical rainforests have the opposite climatic conditions from polar areas. However, they are similar to cold regions in that they are also experiencing rapid changes. Humans have destroyed huge numbers of trees in the rainforests, and this is causing the climate to change.

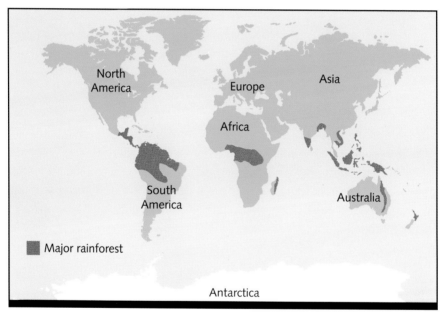

This map shows the distribution of rainforests around the world.

Sources of life

Humans need oxygen to live. We get oxygen from the air when we breathe in. When we breathe out, we emit carbon dioxide and other waste products. Plants do the opposite by taking in carbon dioxide and emitting oxygen. That is one reason why rooms filled with healthy plants feel so refreshing. They are actually cleaning the air that we breathe.

Rainforests have the largest percentage of plant life per square mile on Earth. They provide our atmosphere with vast quantities of oxygen. By destroying huge amounts of rainforest, humans are changing the way our atmosphere operates and also altering the climate.

Interrupting nature

The water cycle describes the way water vapor turns into precipitation and then returns to water vapor. Heat from the Sun causes moisture to evaporate and rise from land and bodies of water. Clouds form in the sky and suspend the particles of water. When the clouds hit cooler air or low-pressure areas, the water becomes heavy and falls as precipitation. Then, the process starts all over again.

Oceans produce a huge amount of the water vapor that forms, but moist rainforests and other plant life also do this. In fact, a great deal of rain that falls on rainforests is generated by water evaporating from its own plants. When trees and other plants are cut down, less rain occurs because there is less water vapor available to form clouds. The effects of this may be global.

Rainforests only cover about 5 percent of Earth's surface, but some scientists estimate they produce 40 percent of Earth's oxygen. Rainforests also support about half of the world's plant and animal species and are sources for 25 percent of the medicines we use.

Protecting rainforests

At one time rainforests covered approximately 14 percent of Earth's surface. Now they cover only about 5 percent. Huge numbers of trees have been cut down for timber and to clear land for farming.

Many organizations and nations are working to protect rainforests. They now realize the value of these regions and fear the consequences of destroying them. Although rainforests are still being cut down, the rate is slower than it was 20 years ago.

Clouds rise from a lush rainforest. Tropical plants absorb some rain, but some precipitation drains into rivers. The remaining moisture evaporates. Disrupting these processes may cause terrible consequences for rainforests. Unfortunately, scientists believe human actions are already causing such disruptions.

"Oceans in Peril: 'We have to change course,' say scientists"

"We have major problems," said Andrew Rosenberg, a member of the president's U.S. Commission on Ocean Policy. "We have to change course." This statement appeared in the *Seattle Times* in February 2004. In 2005 the journal *Science* reported that climate change was triggering new outbreaks of disease in marine environments, affecting everything from coral reefs to oysters. What is the story behind this news?

Almost 70 percent of Earth's surface is covered by ocean. There is a complex, but important, relationship between climate change and processes taking place in oceans.

Currents and climate

Ocean currents can affect a place's climate. They form when there is uneven heating of Earth. Water in the ocean flows when cold water sinks and warm water rises. Cool and warm currents change the temperature of air circulating above them, warming or cooling it. When winds blow onto nearby lands, the lands are also therefore cooled or warmed.

Much of Europe depends on the Gulf Stream current. This current starts in warm water areas near the Gulf of Mexico and flows over 3,000 miles (4,800 kilometers) toward the United Kingdom and Europe, retaining much of its heat. The Gulf Stream causes temperatures in the United Kingdom and western parts of Europe to be relatively warm, considering their northern locations. These areas experience temperatures similar to places located much closer to the equator.

Some experts say that waters from the melting Arctic ice cap could change the Gulf Stream so that it no longer flows toward Europe. The result could be much colder temperatures and a "mini-ice age" for the United Kingdom and Western Europe.

Water vapor

Much of Earth's precipitation results from ocean evaporation. Large amounts of cloud form over oceans every day, and winds carry them toward land areas. Most of the greenhouse effect is actually caused by water vapor. If global warming continues, both precipitation and water vapor processes will change. It could cause climate shifts, such as the Sahara becoming a moist area while the Amazon Rainforest turns into a desert.

Sea creatures depend on specific water temperatures to live. Quick or drastic climate change could destroy many of them. However, the biggest result of global warming, or other climate changes, may be totally unexpected. It is very difficult to predict how changes may affect the weather.

A small portion of the Great Barrier Reef of Australia is shown here. This coral reef is over 1,000 miles (1,600 kilometers) long and contains diverse aquatic life. Coral needs exactly the right amounts of sunlight, heat, and water conditions to thrive.

EL NIÑO AND LA NIÑA

El Niño and La Niña are two ocean currents that directly affect global weather. El Niño currents have caused very rainy conditions and even serious flooding for much of the United States. La Niña currents have had the opposite effect, causing serious droughts. Climatologists worry that global warming might make currents like El Niño and La Niña more extreme. This could cause weather-related disasters in parts of the United States and South America.

More global warming, more hurricanes?

Statistics show that the number of hurricanes and **typhoons** that happen in the world each year has stayed the same for hundreds of years. In recent years, however, the number of powerful hurricanes has begun to rise. In 2004 four major hurricanes swept destructively through Florida. Though loss of life was low, property loss was very high. This was one of the most active years for hurricanes in recent history.

Unfortunately, 2005 was even worse. For the first time since detailed records were kept, all the letters in alphabetic order from A to Z were used to name hurricanes. Hurricanes Katrina and Rita both reached category 5 levels, the strongest rating a hurricane can have. Both weakened before they reached the land, but they still caused tremendous destruction.

Effects of Hurricane Katrina

Hurricane Katrina was the most costly hurricane in U.S. history. High waves called a **storm surge** crashed into Mississippi and Louisiana's coasts on the Gulf of Mexico. Many towns were completely destroyed as powerful waters shattered homes, buildings, and roads. The destruction covered hundreds of square miles.

Walls called levees surround New Orleans. They protect the city from areas where the water level is higher than the land. Hurricanes Katrina and Rita caused powerful waves to crash into these levees. Some broke, and the entire city became flooded.

New Orleans, Louisiana, is located 100 miles (160 kilometers) away from the Gulf Coast, but most of it lies below sea level. Its flood protection is a complicated **levee** and pumping system. Hurricane Katrina's storm surge washed into canals, nearby Lake Pontchartrain, and the Mississippi River, which curves through the city. The river levees held, but a levee on one of the canals and one on the lake broke. Water streamed into the city, overwhelming the pumping system.

Almost all of the 1.3 million residents fled. Hundreds who stayed behind died. Hundreds of thousands lost their homes, and billions of dollars' worth of water damage was caused. After the floods, an organism called **black mold** grew in many structures and caused even more damage.

Louisiana and Mississippi's Gulf Coast communities also suffered huge losses. Buildings, roads, and communication facilities were destroyed. Many miles of coastline were washed away, which meant it was impossible to rebuild some places.

A major reason so many lives were lost was that the hurricane suddenly changed its course. It was not predicted to strike the area until 48 hours before it came ashore. People had little time to board up their homes, gather possessions, and quickly leave. Emergency services were caught off guard and, as a result, were unable to save many people. In addition, some of the levee failures were caused by flaws in their construction. Plans for improving hurricane safety for New Orleans had been proposed, but government bodies voted against them, saying the measures were too expensive.

Scientists say that unusually high water temperatures in the Gulf of Mexico were the major factor causing hurricanes Katrina and Rita to strengthen. Some people wonder if human actions involved with global warming caused the very high water temperatures.

HURRICANE FORMATION

Hurricanes form in warm ocean areas near the equator. They are swirling masses of wind that organize and begin to make large circular paths. Most Atlantic hurricanes start near the west coast of Africa or in warm Caribbean waters. As a hurricane moves, it can strengthen as it passes over warm waters.

HUMANS AND CLIMATE CHANGE

"Climate Change Laid to Humans: Report Warns There's 'no doubt' Industry Is Primary Cause"

On December 4, 2003, the *San Francisco Chronicle* reported: "Thomas Karl, a meteorologist at the National Climatic Data Center in Asheville, N.C., and Kevin Trenberth, chief of the climate analysis section at the National Center for Atmospheric Research [said], . . . '[T]here is no doubt that the composition of the atmosphere is changing because of human activities.'"

Greenhouse gases

Scientists believe that several factors can cause climate change. These include: volcanic action, types of ocean currents, sunspots, greenhouse gases present in the atmosphere, and slight "wobbles" (called **oscillations**) of Earth on its axis. The one humans have some control over is the amount of greenhouse gases in the atmosphere.

Fossil fuels, such as coal, gas, and oil, began to be used in larger amounts in the mid-1800s. **Internal combustion engines**, which power cars, trucks, trains, many factory machines, and some power plants, use fossil fuels for energy. Greenhouse gases have built up at a steadily higher rate as humans have increasingly burned fossil fuels.

The gases are causing a greenhouse effect and rising air temperatures around the world. Some scientists say Earth is warming anyway because of a natural climate cycle. They point to

According to a 2004 article in the *Boston Globe*, cars cause a large percentage of harmful greenhouse gases. For example, measurements show that 40 percent of the greenhouse gases emitted in California come from cars.

Remote mountain areas of the western United States often have clean, clear air. They are far from polluted urban areas. However, winds sometimes carry **pollutants** great distances, and they can cause damage far from the original source.

water vapor, which is almost all caused naturally, as the main source of greenhouse gases. They say that there is more carbon dioxide emitted from volcanoes than from human activity. These scientists believe Earth will adapt naturally, as it has done in the past. For example, after each ice age, temperatures gradually returned to normal and then stayed warmer than average for several years.

Other experts say that Earth's natural processes will not adjust, and that disaster looms. They believe pollution caused by humans has resulted in atmospheric changes that are more serious than those occurring in past ages.

Problems for humans

In England when residents of London took a breath 500 years ago, they inhaled 30 percent less carbon dioxide than people living there today. The air was much cleaner due to the lack of motor vehicles and industrialization.

Although carbon dioxide makes up a tiny percentage of the atmosphere compared with water vapor, scientists have noticed it causing significant changes. Increases in global warming appear directly related to increased **emissions** of carbon dioxide from the burning of fossil fuels in the last 150 years. Health problems, such as skin cancer and increased cases of influenza caused by extremes in weather, are the immediate effects.

EFFECTS OF GREENHOUSE GASES

Greenhouse gases got their name because they thicken the atmosphere and prevent heat from escaping—like a greenhouse. Meanwhile, they still allow heat from the Sun to enter. Some of these gases are harming important layers in the atmosphere. In some cases, these layers are being destroyed. There is a hole in the ozone layer above Antarctica and also a small thinning over the Arctic.

Getting tough on air pollution

In the 1800s, the **Industrial Revolution** began. This involved the widespread use of machines for many jobs. These machines were—and still are—often powered by burning fossil fuels. Unfortunately, machines are not able to burn all of the fossil fuels they use. As a result, harmful chemicals are emitted. The soot and dirt released into the air make their way into Earth's atmosphere. The particles trap heat and cause extra global warming. Scientists disagree on exactly how much fossil fuels raise global temperatures.

Health problems

People inhale harmful substances every day, but more so in heavily industrial areas. If winds do not blow these substances out, or spread them, air pollution can build into an **inversion**. This can cause serious health problems. People with lung problems must breathe harder in order to supply their body with enough oxygen. People with weak hearts are strained because their heart beats more quickly in the hotter conditions that exist during inversions.

Geography can make some cities more prone to air pollution problems than others. Mexico City is in a valley surrounded on three sides by mountains. The mountains block winds from removing harmful substances, making Mexico City one of the world's most polluted cities.

Controversy

Modern industrial nations produce the most air pollution. Waste from factory chimneys, car exhausts, and other sources empty into the atmosphere and add to the greenhouse effect. Scientists have called for all nations to reduce their greenhouse gas emissions because of potential damage to Earth's atmosphere and climate.

POLLUTED CITIES

The following are the cities with the worst air pollution:
1. Delhi, India
2. Beijing, China
3. Calcutta, India
4. Tianjin, China
5. Mexico City, Mexico

The most polluted cities are in nations that are trying to quickly increase industrial output. They usually have few laws regulating pollution levels. In February 2006 journalist Zijun Li wrote: "A recent study by a Chinese research institute found that 400,000 premature deaths are caused every year in China by diseases linked to air pollution. And China's Ministry of Science and Technology reports that 50,000 newborn babies are killed by air pollution a year."

The United States is the biggest greenhouse gas emitter in the world. The United States and a few nations have resisted cutting down on emissions because leaders say it will ruin their economies. In 2002 President George W. Bush's White House press secretary said, "The president is very concerned about the effect Kyoto [an international agreement to reduce greenhouse gases] would have on America's workers, on American jobs, and on the American economy." For example, President Bush estimated that 4.9 million U.S. workers would lose their jobs if the country tried to meet the international goals set by the Kyoto Agreement (see pages 40–41).

President Bush has only asked U.S. companies to voluntarily reduce harmful emissions. Some measures, such as production of cleaner-burning car engines, have been implemented, but scientists say more should be done. They say that decreasing the amount of health problems and preventing disastrous weather events will save money in the long term if more is done to reduce greenhouse gas emissions.

Particles released in smoke from chimneys like this are believed to be the main source of both acid rain and global warming. Chimney filters and scrubbers can trap several pollutants, but they are expensive.

Since 1973 Iceland's Breidemerkurjokull Glacier has been quickly melting. NASA scientists say it is shrinking by 2 percent each year. Global warming is occurring more quickly in polar areas than other regions of Earth and endangering Arctic people's way of life.

Saving Arctic people

For thousands of years, native people of the Arctic, such as Inuits and Samis, have lived unique lifestyles. These lifestyles depend on a consistently cold climate, however, and now climate change is threatening their whole way of life.

Arctic struggles

There have been people living in Arctic regions for many years. In northern Siberia, Alaska, Scandinavia, and Canada people mine, fish, and hunt for a living. Little farming can be done, so Arctic people depend on fishing, hunting, and imported foods for nutrition. Often they have to travel far, across large patches of ice, to hunt and fish. These expeditions are becoming dangerous and unsuccessful because of climate changes. This is because the ice forms later in the year and melts earlier. Coastlines that used to be frozen have now eroded. As a result, many native homes on coastlines have been destroyed when soil beneath them loosens. Warmer conditions have also caused swarms of mosquitoes to infest villages and to drive off wildlife. Several hunters have drowned in icy waters when unusually thin ice collapsed beneath them. Wildlife, including polar bears and caribou, is dying out because it cannot adapt to the increasing temperatures.

The Arctic is also particularly sensitive to pollution. High concentrations of **toxic** chemicals have been found in the meat of the animals Arctic people consume. Experts believe that winds are transporting harmful pollutants to these areas. Pregnant women in the Arctic have been advised not to eat meat killed in local hunts.

Climate change and human rights

Inuit people have begun to take action. They formed a group to represent 150,000 Arctic people living in Canada, Russia, Greenland, and the United States to try to save their lifestyles. Their main target is the biggest emitter of greenhouse gases in the world: the United States. Inuits believe the pollution caused by the United States, along with the country's unwillingness to make changes, is wiping out Arctic cultures.

Inuit people filed a petition in 2005 to a large group of nations that met to discuss climate change. Martin Wagner, a lawyer for the Inuit, said, "[The petition makes a] connection between climate change and human rights . . . [The Inuit's] ability to maintain their unique culture, which is absolutely dependent on ice and snow; their ability to hunt and fish . . . their ability to have shelter and build their homes—all of those rights are impacted by climate change in the Arctic."

So far the United States has not offered a response to the Inuit petition. Meanwhile, Arctic people hope that their climate will not be so damaged that it cannot be saved.

Caribou travel hundreds, even thousands, of miles each year in search of pastures. Climate change has altered their travel and feeding patterns. Large numbers of these grand animals will die unless the current pattern of warmer climates is reversed.

Fatal suntans and sickness

The atmosphere surrounding Earth contains several substances and a series of different layers. Each layer is made up of slightly different things and has a different purpose. The ozone layer protects living organisms on Earth from powerful **ultraviolet-B rays** (UV-B rays).

Helpful sunlight

Most of the Sun's rays are helpful and warm our planet. For example, they promote plant growth for valuable crops and forests. Some of the Sun's rays are the basis for the vitamin D formation that helps humans maintain high energy levels.

UV-B rays have some constructive uses. Doctors and biologists make use of ultraviolet rays to kill certain types of bacteria and germs. In some cases, they need to do this for medical procedures or experiments. Long-term exposure to UV-B, however, can cause skin cancers.

Sunbathers must beware of increasingly dangerous ultraviolet rays. Thinning layers of Earth's atmosphere allow intense sunlight to strike Earth. Doctors blame this for the increase in cases of skin damage and of deadly skin cancer.

Dangerous rays

A dangerous activity of many people is to sunbathe at every opportunity. Exposing human skin to ultraviolet rays for long periods can literally "kill" skin cells and promote deadly skin cancer.

The combined effects of UV-B rays with Earth's thinning atmosphere are putting millions at risk. Skin cancer is on the rise because suntans have become more popular, while at the same time exposing skin to the Sun has become more dangerous. This trend began about 30 years ago. According to the American Cancer Society, skin cancer cases have increased by eight times during that period! People who are outside for extended periods need to use sunblock or wear more protective clothing.

Heat and disease

The damage to certain layers in the atmosphere is also affecting people's health in other ways. The increasing global temperatures can cause sickness and disease. Heat is a **catalyst**: it speeds up reactions and promotes growth. Harmful viruses multiply and become stronger more quickly in hot conditions.

Tropical areas of Asia, Africa, and South America have struggled with rising cases of serious diseases. As more people and goods travel to destinations around the world, these diseases can spread more easily. Scientists worry about pandemics. These are devastating diseases that spread over a large region of the world. Scientists fear diseases may spread more quickly because of the warmer average temperatures on Earth.

8,000-YEAR WARM-UP?

Some scientists report that global warming began 8,000 years ago. Their study was based on the study of ice cores, which are deep cuts of ice from glaciers and ice caps. Ice core evidence comes from winds and water moving materials from all over Earth, which settle in ice during various times. Some scientists say that global warming began at the same time farmers began cutting down more trees and doing more farming 8,000 years ago.

"When I was a child . . . "

"I'm 37, and live in Slovakia, Central Europe. I can say the weather in the last 10 or 12 years is different than before. Winters in my childhood were very cold with a lot of snow. Now a week or two are pretty cold but there is almost no snow" (Cyril Hajik, Slovakia). What is the story behind this news?

Descriptions of climate change come not only from scientists, but from all people. Many times we hear stories of past winters and legendary snows. More and more, people find these memories are accurate and provide personal evidence of climate change. Often, personal recollections can give us a good view of past climatic conditions. It appears that people from all over the world believe global warming is taking place.

In 2004 wildfires burned over 5 million acres (2 million hectares) of forest in Alaska. Many local people believe that these fires—driven by unusually hot, dry weather and lightning strikes—show that climate change is happening.

Weather diaries

Weather diaries can be valuable. Climatologists record statistics and write accounts from a scientific viewpoint. When we use personal accounts, we can see more detailed descriptions of how climate affected people.

For example, a climatologist may report that on January 27, 1964, the temperature in Oymyakon, Russia, was –58 °F (–50 °C). These figures tell us it was cold, but descriptions do even more. A person living in the area could tell us that uncovered skin could be frostbitten within 15 minutes; that water poured from an insulated container froze before hitting the ground and rolled away in solid balls of ice; and—if conditions stayed the same for a few weeks—that rivers froze to be so thick that vehicles could drive on them.

The mountains of Juneau, Alaska, used to be covered with snow. For years the state of Alaska has seen a steady decline in the amount of snow it receives.

Global warming: Personal accounts

Robert Skilling of Hingham, Massachusetts, kept a diary of the weather in the Boston area up until 1954. His diary and other records kept by private citizens assist climatologists. Sometimes they record information that professionals missed, or they wrote data in ways that improved understanding.

According to an article in the *Boston Globe*, Skilling's diary "noted subtle changes in the local weather that reflect a worldwide trend: a slow drift toward warmer temperatures."

Mickey Lesley and Margo Waring live in Juneau, Alaska. Mickey wrote: "We didn't shovel snow once the past two winters and have shoveled very infrequently since 1992. . . . Until the early '70s it snowed through the first week of May [in Juneau]. We don't get snow in the spring at all now."

KEEPING A WEATHER DIARY

Many people record weather conditions as a hobby. A few basic instruments are needed to do this:

- Thermometer for temperatures
- Barometer to measure air pressure
- Rain gauge to measure precipitation
- Weather vane to show wind direction
- Anemometer to find wind speed.

A hygrometer or psychrometer measures relative humidity, but this is more difficult to obtain.

Nations take action

Almost every nation on Earth wants to prevent air pollution and global warming. The problem is that doing this may cost money in the short term. There will be long-term benefits, but it is sometimes hard to make people see the significance of this.

Many nations have taken steps to reduce global warming and harmful air pollution. Some countries originally took measures to provide a cleaner, healthier environment, but have now added efforts to reduce climate change.

Companies clean up

One international company, E. I. du Pont de Nemours and Company, decreased its greenhouse gas emissions by 72 percent, still increased its production, and saved more than $2 billion in the past 10 years. Together, a computer company, pharmaceutical firm, and three other companies saved billions of dollars by reducing carbon dioxide emissions. Several other large businesses have said they will take similar actions and use energy more efficiently. They know higher profits will be the result.

Many of the methods these companies used were very simple. Companies upgraded electric wires and control boxes to conserve great amounts of power and reduce electricity bills. They used more fuel-efficient vehicles for company transportation to save gasoline.

The clean air of Perth is a symbol of Australia's commitment to fight greenhouse gas emissions. Australia's government has pledged to surpass international goals for decreasing air pollution.

Government actions

Some nations give tax breaks to companies and individuals who do a good job conserving energy and penalize those who do not. There is also funding for research to find new types of energy and better ways of conserving important natural resources. Nations encourage the use of non-polluting solar, wind, and water power. Additionally, leaders of nations have called on citizens to help in the fight to stop pollution and the build-up of waste that affects global warming.

Poorer nations have also begun to act. They know that using good methods to prevent air pollution and climate change will help them in the long term. For example, they will save on energy costs. These nations have taken measures themselves and joined in international moves to cooperate in reducing greenhouse gas emissions.

Several meetings have taken place to decide on and enforce global agreements to stop climate change caused by human activity.

German Chancellor Angela Merkel makes a presentation at an international conference. Germany is proud of its success in reducing greenhouse gases. The industrial Ruhr Valley region of Germany used to release huge amounts of pollutants, but it has substantially reduced these emissions.

LEADING THE EFFORT

Germany is a leading nation in reducing greenhouse gas emissions and is the world's leading nation in using wind for energy. The government has also:
- Closed factories that caused heavy pollution
- Made laws that require cars to use fuels that create less pollution
- Insisted on the use of improved technology to reduce harmful car emissions
- Reduced taxes for companies that use natural gas and other clean fuels
- Encouraged the use of hydroelectric power (using water to generate electricity, rather than burning fossil fuels).

International debate

Although scientists issued warnings many years ago, the **Kyoto Protocol** began the first serious attempt to stop global warming. According to a headline on the CBC News website in September 2002, opponents said, "Consumers will feel the pinch of Kyoto." In the same article, a Canadian business leader agreed with the Kyoto Protocol: "Les Steel, president of the Alberta Federation of Labou, says the agreement will save what resources are left in the world. 'Bringing the Kyoto Accord in, and doing some other measures as well, is a way of preserving our environment and making sure our resources are sustainable,' said Steel." What is the story behind this news?

International conferences

By 1977 several studies concluded that CFCs were destroying the ozone layer. This led to a special conference of United Nations members in 1978 at which they banned the use of CFCs in aerosols. The United Nations Environment Program Conference also urged international studies of atmospheric processes.

A series of international conferences were held in the following years at Montréal in Canada, Rio de Janeiro in Brazil, Vienna in Austria, and other locations. Information was shared and proposals were made to limit air pollution that harms Earth's atmosphere and results in climate change.

Kyoto Protocol

In 1997 the most important international action to stop global warming occurred. Representatives of nations from around the world met in Kyoto, Japan, to set specific goals and carry out a plan to reduce greenhouse gas emissions. This agreement set specific targets for nations to reduce air pollution by the year 2010. The targets would be accomplished by emitting less carbon dioxide and other greenhouse gases. In addition, it outlined a plan to help poorer nations reduce air pollution.

President George W. Bush makes a speech in Columbus, Ohio, in which he describes his energy policy. President Bush believes international cooperation to reduce greenhouse gases is unfair to the United States. He wants U.S. industry to voluntarily reduce harmful emissions.

About 100 nations signed the Kyoto Protocol, including the United States—although the U.S. later rejected the protocol. U.S. leaders decided that meeting the terms of Kyoto would damage the U.S. economy. This was a serious setback for the agreement because the U.S. is one of the richest nations in the world. It is also the world's biggest emitter of greenhouse gases.

Despite U.S. disapproval, the other countries that signed are trying to implement the plan, and people around the world seem to support this. However, nations are having difficulty meeting many of the Kyoto Protocol's targets. Between 1997 and 2006, there were eight conferences held by participants in the Kyoto Protocol. These nations have struggled to improve the agreement and their efforts to reduce greenhouse gas emissions.

KYOTO: DIFFERENT PERSPECTIVES

There are several arguments for and against the Kyoto Protocol.

Supporters of Kyoto say the benefits of the agreement are that it:

- Gives nations the opportunity to work together, which is the only way to reduce greenhouse gas emissions globally
- Motivates nations to reduce greenhouse gases by giving them specific targets for improvement
- Encourages energy efficiency
- Offers long-term benefits and savings.

Opponents of Kyoto say the problems with the agreement are that it:

- Is not as important without the participation of the United States, which is the largest producer of greenhouse gas emissions and has vast resources to assist the international effort
- Has targets that are too low and that need to be increased significantly to have an impact on global warming. U.S. leaders have also stated that Kyoto's targets are more difficult for larger nations to meet.
- Has no punishments if targets are not met
- Is too expensive in the short term, according to U.S. leaders.

Public support

In July 2005 a detailed **public opinion poll** on climate change was conducted in the United States. An organization called Program on International Policy Attitudes found that Americans overwhelmingly favored policies to limit greenhouse gas emissions. Still, President Bush and other leaders of the government refused to accept the Kyoto Protocol.

Protestors in Montréal, Canada, call for more action to prevent global warming. The protest took place at the same time as a United Nations conference on climate change. Similar demonstrations have taken place in many nations around the world.

Poll results

The poll found that 94 percent of Americans believed the United States should limit its greenhouse gas emissions at least as much as other modern nations. Almost half, 44 percent, believed the United States should do more than average. In the same survey, 73 percent of Americans said the United States should "participate in the Kyoto Protocol to reduce global warming."

President Bush and other U.S. leaders said that following the Kyoto Protocol would damage the U.S. economy. Yet 71 percent of Americans taking part in the 2005 poll believed the U.S. economy would become more competitive worldwide if it followed the Kyoto Protocol. In fact, 56 percent of Americans in the poll said they favored taking high-cost steps to halt global warming.

Scientists were asked: "Is global warming or climate change due to the build-up of greenhouse gases?" Of the scientists polled, 72 percent said a great deal of or some climate change was due to these gases building up.

Designing polls

We all like to know what other people are thinking and to see if their opinions match ours. As polls have become more accurate and easier to distribute to masses of people, they have become more influential. There are many instances when government leaders have changed policies because of results they saw in public opinion polls.

Media sources make frequent use of polls because of the interest polls attract. Polls do not ask the opinions of everyone in a nation, but instead use small groups called **samples**. When a sample is picked correctly, the small number of people polled represent a wide variety of beliefs, backgrounds, and other characteristics. In this way they can accurately portray a much larger population.

DESIGNING YOUR OWN SURVEY

Designing a survey to find out other people's opinions can be a challenge. Start with a **hypothesis** (an educated guess) concerning how people feel about an issue. To collect usable data, questions should be relatively simple and have short answers. Questions with "yes" or "no" answers allow you to obtain definite results that can be easily compared. Of course, the hardest part is deciding exactly what to ask.

Opponents of global warming theories

Some scientists do not believe there is enough proof that current climate changes are serious, or that human activity is a major factor. Has the media made people believe that the situation is worse than it really is? Or are we only just finding out about important scientific discoveries, now that the issue of climate change is popular with the public?

Predicting climate change

Polls are not always right, and sometimes the majority opinion is the wrong one. Some experts do not agree with the current majority opinion on global warming.

Much evidence of harmful climate change has been gathered in polar regions. Scientists such as Dr. Sallie Baliunas, the Enviro-Science Editor at tcsdaily.com, say the Arctic climate is very complex and varies dramatically from region to region. She says that it is almost impossible to predict how climate change will progress worldwide by studying Arctic regions alone.

According to Dr. S. Fred Singer, a physicist at George Mason University in Fairfax, Virginia, the main reason for current global warming has little to do with human activities. Dr. Singer states that factors such as water vapor, volcanic activity, and oscillations occur naturally and cause much more global warming than the greenhouse gases produced by human activity. There are also records in Earth's past of quicker and larger climate changes than anything being predicted right now. Earth and its inhabitants recovered from all of these.

Gathering evidence

Urban areas of the world have experienced a warming climate in recent years. However, some scientists say this should not lead to conclusions that the whole Earth is warming. Measurements have been taken at several sites along Greenland's coast. A team of experts from the Los Alamos [New Mexico] National Laboratory conducted these tests. They concluded that Greenland coastal areas have experienced a cooling trend since 1940.

Many predictions of disastrous warming are based on past climatic events. Some scientists say there have been short, rapid warming trends in the past that had opposite effects from what is now being predicted. For example, from 1900 to 1940 there were times when significant warming took place. According to most scientists, this should cause ice to melt and ocean levels to rise. However, the opposite occurred: ice is less dense than water, so when ice in the sea melts, sea levels actually drop.

Global warming is thought to have increased the amount of moisture in the air. This has caused an increase in snowfall over Antarctica.

Popular beliefs vs. accuracy

These "opposing scientists" believe that more studies are needed before conclusions can be reached. They say: "Why invest time, money, and effort to prevent disasters that may not happen?" In an interview, Dr. Singer said that certain scientists "have a particular point of view" and that they ignore important factors in order to prove their point. Popular views can mislead people as to what is actually true. In the 1400s, for example, most people believed Earth was flat.

CLIMATE CHANGE OR TEMPORARY CONDITION?

There are indications that several climate changes happening right now are short term and local, rather than long term and global. For example, ocean currents in the Pacific Ocean have recently changed and caused much warmer conditions in Alaska. Dr. S. Frank Singer and others say that this is a relatively short-term situation, and not a sign of climate change. El Niño and La Niña ocean currents (see pages 24–25) fall into the same category.

Climate change predictions

Like weather, climate is difficult to predict. Scientists have predicted a wide variety of outcomes concerning climate change, but the main concern for the future is the effect that pollution will have. Will global warming cause floods, expansion of deserts, or an ice age? Could all of these negative predictions be wrong and the global climate simply correct itself? Experts are trying to answer these questions.

Warnings

Scientists warn us to be careful about what we release into the atmosphere. They believe Earth could be seriously harmed because it can only deal with a certain amount of pollution. They warn that if pollution levels go beyond certain limits, extremely dangerous climate changes may occur.

These Polish students from the Bialowieza Forestry School are examining ferns. More and more colleges around the world are offering courses that study how to protect Earth's environment.

Polar disasters

One predicted outcome of pollution is that more and more greenhouse gases will build up and raise temperatures by holding warm air near Earth's surface. If Antarctica's ice cap were to melt completely, coastal areas would be flooded. This would be disastrous for the large number of cities and people located on coasts.

An opposite outcome is possible. Some experts believe that global warming could plunge Earth into a sudden ice age. This would occur if greenhouse gases caused higher amounts of ocean water to evaporate and form massive amounts of cloud. The result would be increased snowfall, which would cause ice caps to expand and send powerful winter storms to the south.

Changing oceans

Climatologists know that oceanic conditions have a major influence on land conditions. Another possible outcome of global warming is that higher ocean temperatures could cause stronger storms. Hurricanes, such as Katrina, have already demonstrated how destructive and deadly they can be. Again, coastal areas would suffer.

Some scientists are concerned that the worldwide warming trend will alter or even stop ocean currents such as the Gulf Stream. Without the warm waters of the Gulf Stream flowing toward it, Europe could experience a sudden ice age.

In the 1970s, many scientists worried that global warming might disrupt weather patterns and cause new deserts to form. This would occur if certain prevailing winds were disrupted. Some experts still believe this could happen.

The unknown

More and more climatologists say the real danger of climate change lies in "the unknown." They wonder if the rise in greenhouse gases may cause totally new problems. Climate change may result in a combination of harmful effects or even something that has never been seen before.

Some cities, such as Venice, Italy, already have problems with coastal flooding. If ocean levels rise due to global warming, similar scenes to this one could occur in many of the world's coastal cities.

EARTH'S WORST DISASTER

The Permian Extinction was Earth's greatest natural disaster. Scientists believe it was caused by volcanoes, climate change, and possibly an asteroid striking Earth 250 million years ago. Numerous volcanic eruptions caused quick build-ups of greenhouse gases. This resulted in sudden changes in the ocean that killed over 90 percent of the world's sea life. These concentrated gases also caused quick climate changes that wiped out over 60 percent of land animals.

Is climate more important than weather?

Newspapers and media sources rarely have "front-page" stories dealing with scientific subjects. Profits driven by the ability to attract readers and viewers is the main reason for this situation. Owners have the right to operate their businesses as they wish, but should more scientific articles appear on the front pages of newspapers? How can scientists and writers make scientific stories more interesting?

Globally, people have to constantly adapt to their natural and man-made environments. Arctic societies blame modern, industrial nations for not only causing damage to Earth's natural processes, but also for destroying their whole way of life. Industrial nations are located thousands of miles from these Arctic societies, but:

- Are Arctic people victims of greenhouse gases that cause global warming?
- Should modern nations compensate them for their losses?

Almost all people realize that destroying rainforests, damaging oceans, and causing more strong hurricanes are things that need to be stopped. The problems are:

- How can rainforests, oceans, and areas prone to hurricanes be protected without spending huge sums of money?
- Which actions are most effective in preventing large amounts of air pollution?

This painting gives an idea of the consequences of a meteor striking Earth 65 million years ago. Scientists believe the meteor crash caused a massive tsunami and hurled dust into the atmosphere. They say there was so much dust that the world's climate changed, and that this contributed to the extinction of dinosaurs.

Car companies are already producing environmentally friendly cars. These cars use alternatives to fossil fuels for their sources of power. The innovative technology will save owners money and protect the atmosphere from harmful greenhouse gas emissions.

Plans to reduce greenhouse gas emissions are at the heart of nations' efforts to prevent harmful climate changes. National leaders and scientists argue about how serious these climate changes are, and how much of an impact human activities are having. International cooperation is taking place, but:

- Can agreements like the Kyoto Protocol solve most of the significant problems related to global warming?
- What are the best arguments to prove global warming is not a major problem?
- Is the current rate of climate change putting Earth in danger?

Earth is a complex living organism—a **biosphere**. Humans have attempted to learn from its past activities and predict its future, but no one knows what will happen next.

In science, there are rules and laws. For example, in physics it has been shown that every action causes an equal and opposite reaction. However, climate and weather have almost endless **variables**, so it is very difficult to make accurate predictions. The world's people hope scientists will soon be able to make these predictions. Preserving life on Earth may be at stake.

FAMOUS RECORD KEEPER

From 1776 until 1816, President Thomas Jefferson recorded daily weather conditions. No matter where he was, he attempted to write down the temperature, wind direction, barometric pressure, and describe the precipitation or humidity levels. He believed his recordings would make it possible to predict the weather.

TIMELINE

1824

French scientist Jean-Baptiste Fourier says there is an atmospheric effect keeping Earth warmer than it should be. He is describing the greenhouse effect.

1861

Irish scientist John Tyndall describes how water vapor can be a greenhouse gas.

1890s

Swedish scientist Svante Arrhenius says burning fossil fuels could lead to global warming.

1890s to 1940

The average surface air temperatures increase by 0.45 °F (0.25 °C). Some scientists see the Dust Bowl as a sign of the greenhouse effect at work.

1940 to 1970

Earth cools by 0.4 °F (0.2 °C) and scientific interest in the greenhouse effect wanes. Some climatologists even predict a new ice age.

1957

U.S. oceanographer Roger Revelle warns that humans are releasing too many greenhouse gases with uncertain effects.

1970s

The U.S. Department of Energy reports increased concerns about future global warming.

1979

The first World Climate Conference says climate change is a major concern. It asks governments to help prevent harmful climate change.

1985

Joseph Farman discovers a hole in the ozone layer.

An international conference at Villach, Austria, warns that greenhouse gases will cause rising, unusually high temperatures.

1987

The warmest year worldwide since records began.

1988

Global warming attracts worldwide headlines after scientists at Congressional hearings in Washington, D.C., blame major U.S. drought on its influence.

A meeting of climate scientists in Toronto, Canada, subsequently calls for 20 percent cuts in global carbon dioxide emissions by the year 2005.

The United Nations sets up the Intergovernmental Panel on Climate Change (IPCC) to analyze and report on scientific findings.

1990

The IPCC finds that the planet has warmed by 0.9 °F (0.5 °C) in the past century and issues warnings to stop the trend.

1991

The Philippine volcano Mount Pinatubo erupts. It throws so much debris into the atmosphere that global temperatures drop for two years.

1992

A Climate Change Convention in Rio de Janeiro, Brazil, agrees to prevent "dangerous" warming from greenhouse gases.

1995

The hottest year recorded to date.

1997

The Kyoto Protocol agrees on legally binding emissions cuts for industrialized nations.

2000

Scientists warn that the world could warm by 11 °F (6 °C) within a century. A series of major floods around the world causes increased public concerns.

2001

President George W. Bush renounces the Kyoto Protocol because he believes it will damage the U.S. economy.

2002

The world experiences the fourth hottest year on record.

2003

Globally it is the third hottest year on record, and Europe experiences the hottest summer for at least 500 years; 30,000 die of heat-related illnesses.

2005

The second hottest year on record, and hurricanes Katrina and Rita cause massive destruction and huge numbers of deaths.

GLOSSARY

baseline average or basic estimate that scientists establish so they can compare other statistical readings to it

bias for or against a particular viewpoint. For example, an article can be biased toward a particular political party.

biosphere total collection of the living organisms on Earth

black mold harmful fungus-like growth that grows in hot, moist conditions

CFCs (chlorofluorocarbons) substances that help aerosol cans operate, but harm Earth's atmosphere when released into the air

carbon dioxide gas released into the air after a chemical reaction that burns or heats oxygen

catalyst object or substance that speeds up a chemical reaction

climate change alteration in long-term average weather conditions

climate cycle repeating trends of climate

climatologist scientist who is a climate expert

desertification climate change that transforms a place into a desert

Dust Bowl prolonged dry weather in the 1930s that caused desert-like conditions to prevail in the midwestern United States

emissions substances discharged into the air

evaporate change from a liquid to a gas

fossil fuels minerals that can produce energy when they are burned. They are made up of ancient, decayed plants and animals.

global warming worldwide pattern of rising temperatures

greenhouse effect situation in which Earth's atmosphere will allow a large portion of the Sun's heat to reach Earth and then prevents it from escaping

greenhouse gas substance released into the atmosphere that allows the Sun's heat to enter, but not to leave very easily

humidity water vapor suspended in the air

hypothesis prediction based on limited research

ice age period during which a large part of Earth was covered in ice

Industrial Revolution time period when people first began making and using power-driven machines to do work on a large scale

internal combustion engine motor with moving parts powered by tiny, heat produced explosions

inversion time in which heavy, cold air holds warm, polluted air near Earth's surface

Kyoto Protocol UN agreement between most of the countries of the world to try to reduce greenhouse gas emissions

levee man-made ridge that protects lands near a body of water from flooding

media means of communication including newspapers, magazines, radio programs, television programs, and the Internet

oscillation slight wobble or movement of Earth as it spins on its axis

ozone layer layer of the atmosphere that stops harmful ultraviolet rays from reaching Earth's surface

pandemic disease that spreads over a very large region of the world, affecting masses of people

pollutant substance that causes pollution

precipitation rain or snow

prevailing wind air current that consistently moves in the same direction

public opinion poll organized survey of people's views or opinions on issues

sample small group of people that is designed to represent a very large group of people

slant particular point of view from which something is seen or presented

storm surge large wave, or waves, of water caused when high winds of a powerful storm "push" water toward a coastline

toxic poisonous

typhoon powerful storm that occurs in regions of the Pacific Ocean that is similar to a hurricane

ultraviolet-B ray light beam from the Sun that is harmful to humans in large doses

urban town or city

variable item in a study that can change

FIND OUT MORE

Books

Bradley, Susannah. *Your Environment: Global Warming*. Mankato, Minn.: Stargazer, 2005.

Brown, Paul. *Face the Facts: Global Pollution*. Chicago: Raintree, 2003.

Chapman, Matthew, and Rob Bowden. *21st Century Debates: Air Pollution*. Chicago: Raintree, 2002.

Corn, John. *Earth's Changing Landscape: Weather and Climate*. Mankato, Minn.: Smart Apple Media, 2004.

Gifford, Clive. *Planet Under Pressure: Pollution*. Chicago: Heinemann Library, 2006.

Harrison, Carol, and David Krasnow. *Weather and Climate*. Milwaukee: Gareth Stevens, 2004.

Inskipp, Carol. *Improving Our Environment: Reducing and Recycling Waste*. Milwaukee: Gareth Stevens, 2005.

Love, Ann, and Jane Drake. *Trash Action: A Fresh Look at Garbage*. Plattsburgh, N.Y.: Tundra, 2006.

Morgan, Sally. *Science at the Edge: Global Warming*. Chicago: Heinemann Library, 2003.

Puay, Lim Cheung. *Green Alert: Our Warm Planet*. Chicago: Raintree, 2004.

Puay, Lim Cheung. *Green Alert: Vanishing Forests*. Chicago: Raintree, 2004.

Scoones, Simon. *21st Century Debates: Climate Change*. Chicago: Raintree, 2002.

Sneddon, Robert. *Essential Energy: Energy from Fossil Fuels*. Chicago: Heinemann Library, 2002.

Websites

www.newscientist.com/channel/earth/climate-change
This part of the New Scientist website focuses on climate change. It includes a timeline and an archive of related articles.

yosemite.epa.gov/oar/globalwarming.nsf/content/index.html
The website of the U.S. Environmental Protection Agency includes information about the potential impact of climate change where you live.

www.globalwarming.org
This contains an archive of articles written about global warming, including many that suggest the threat has been exaggerated. The site is run by the Cooler Heads Coalition, a group that formed out of a "concern that the American people were not being informed about the economic impact of proposals to drastically reduce greenhouse gas emissions."

www.climatehotmap.org
A map of the world showing where unusual climate conditions have been observed recently.

www.worldviewofglobalwarming.org
A collection of photographs that demonstrate some of the effects of global warming.

www.greenpeace.org/usa/campaigns/global-warming-and-energy
Read how Greenpeace is taking action against some of the causes of climate change.

Activities

Here are some topics to research if you want to find out more about global warming:

- Population growth

- Alternative energy sources

- How an increase in greenhouse gases leads to higher temperatures

- The harmful effects of aircraft pollution

- Ways in which you can reduce your carbon "footprint"

- Species threatened by climate change.

INDEX